Inciden't Management nt

For I.T. Departments

...in 10 Easy Steps

Darren O'Toole

ISBN: 978-1511631747

First Edition

A Note from the Author

"Mine is not to reason why, merely reboot and then retry!"

As an Information Technology leader with over 30 years of experience, the one recurring thing I have learned in my career is that Management, and the user community, does not like system outages!

As members of the I.T. Department, our obligation is to respond to outages quickly and get systems back up and running again A.S.A.P!

In ten simple steps this book lays out the foundations of a successful Incident Management program that can be implemented quickly and easily in your company. All of the suggestions are based on ITIL methodologies, but add in real world experience and expand on areas where ITIL doesn't go into detail.

Take this and make it your own. Use it with your I.T. teams and share it with I.T. Leadership. The end result will be quicker resolution of incidents and a better overall end user experience.

Best Regards,

Darren O'Toole

Contents

Step 1: Incident Management - What it is and What it is not

So what exactly is "Incident Management" and why are we so concerned about it?

At its very core, Incident Management is a well thought out process that defines exactly how to evaluate and respond to an unplanned interruption to an I.T. service. The unexpected interruption may, or may not, have caused a reduction in quality of service, but there is currently adverse risk to the user experience. By following a well defined Incident Management process you will have the fastest possible mean time to resolution, which minimizes the negative user experience.

The value proposition is that an effective Incident Management program can have a major impact on the overall I.T. customer satisfaction levels of the company. It can also play a big part in the company's bottom line by significantly reducing downtime and it's associated expenses. Effective Incident Management also ensures you are meeting the agreed to service levels with the business.

As an example, imagine working for a very large customer service call center company. A network outage means that thousands of agents can no longer take customer phone calls. The financial penalties for this, plus the negative perception of I.T., are significant. Even a short outage can result in thousands of dollars in lost revenue. Having a good Incident Management program in place ensures there is always the shortest mean time to resolution of outages.

In another example, imagine you are working for a manufacturer of heart valves. A system outage can stop products from shipping, which in turn delays heart valves being delivered to hospitals. This has the very real possibility of impacting life saving surgeries. Again, quickly responding to incidents, while being thoroughly prepared, helps ensure systems are brought back online as quick as possible.

Incident Management is all about deploying a plan of action to resolve unexpected events and get services running again as quickly as possible. While this sounds simple enough, many I.T. departments struggle with putting together a plan. Instead, there is usually chaos and confusion when a system goes down. No one knows who is responsible, minutes and hours are wasted in slow troubleshooting and often, there is backlash afterwards because the right people were not involved.

To help clarify, Incident Management is not root cause analysis, it is not problem management, it is not change management, and it is not even about finding a permanent solution. These are all separate processes that have different intentions. For example, Problem Management, another ITIL process, focuses on finding the root cause of an incident, or recurring problem. I discuss this in detail in my Problem Management book. Incident Management is all about getting systems back up and running quickly, which may even include temporary workarounds.

So how is an incident different from a service request? The difference is the surprise factor! If you are surprised that something is not working as expected, it is probably an incident. If it is a request for an enhancement or something new and different, then it is probably a service request. In this book we will be focused on incidents, and more specifically, major incidents that will engage your Incident Management process.

Why is it important to understand what Incident Management is not? Because focusing on the wrong thing during an outage burns valuable time. Too often, I.T. teams will get too far into the weeds during an outage conducting deep root cause analysis or trying to build a permanent solution. I suggest that good notes be taken during an outage and that a meeting be set up afterwards to determine the root cause of the outage and additional resolution steps. While the business is impacted by an incident the goal must be to get systems functioning and minimize the adverse impact quickly.

Therefore, the first step to a successful Incident Management program is to recognize what the intention of this important process is (quick resolution) and to understand that a simple, but effective, Incident Management program needs to be put in place soonest! By taking the first step and learning about Incident Management you are off to a great start!

It is important to note that developing an Incident Management strategy cannot be undertaken alone. It is a process that impacts all I.T. departments and needs the full support of executive management. It also needs the support of each individual I.T. team. By understanding the value of such a process, and by being able to articulate that value to management, you can get the support and buy-in you need for your Incident Management program.

Now that you understand what Incident Management is, I would also like to call out the ITIL Incident Management process flow, shown below. ITIL has done a nice job of identifying each of the key steps in a formal Incident Management program and I fully support their model. What I would like to achieve with this book is to build upon their model with real world information, based on many years of experience. Use what ITIL provides, along with my recommendations here, to build out your own successful program.

ITIL's Incident Management Process Flow:

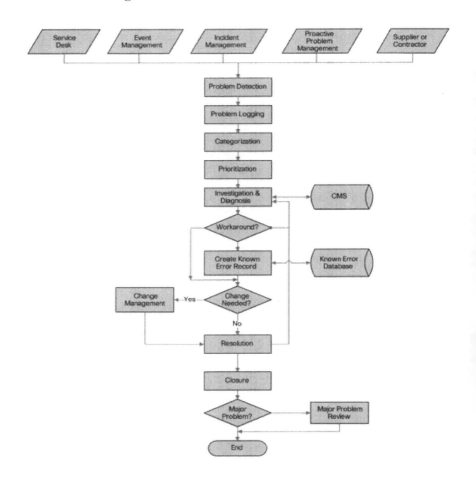

Step 2: Role Play - Who Does What?

Now that you've decided to implement an Incident Management program, who are the key players, who is responsible for what, who owns this process, and how is it supported globally, 24x7? All great questions!

The most important role in your new Incident Management process is the **Incident Manager**. This person could be described as the leader of the pack, the driver of getting you to a resolution, the one who takes charge and gets things fixed quickly.

In smaller companies, this person may be the I.T. Manager or Senior Technician, while in larger companies it may be a full-time role. In multinational companies this role may pass from person to person around the globe in a "follow-the-sun" model.

The important thing is that someone has to step up and take ownership of an incident. If not, people will flounder around, not sure what they are supposed to be doing, burning valuable time and extending the adverse impact to your customers.

When teaching this course in the corporate world I often joke that this role is perfectly suited for those individuals who tend to be outspoken and somewhat bossy! The reason I say this is that the Incident Manager has to be comfortable asking people to take action, dealing with difficult vendors, or escalating to the most senior levels of management. A take charge attitude goes a long way in this role.

Finding just the right candidate for this role is critical. It's definitely possible to train someone for the Incident Management role, but they must be given full support as they develop this skill set. They also need authority to follow the process, which might mean making critical decisions, calling people in to work after hours, escalating support calls with vendors, or spending money to fix issues. I also recommend the person in this role attend the ITIL Foundation training. This will give them a basic understanding across all of the ITIL processes, many of which can be applied to Incident Management.

The next role to address is the **I.T. Technician**. This is the person who is actually working the problem and trying to resolve the issue. I mention this role even though it may seem obvious. The reason is that Technicians need to be managed in a certain way during an incident.

First, they need to be given enough breathing room to do their jobs. Let them stay focused on fixing the issue, while other people help by providing status updates, or engaging with vendors etc. Too often, a Technician gets distracted with a barrage of questions and loses his or her train of thought, resulting in slower resolution.

One important note to keep in mind with Technicians, and something we address in the SLA section, is that at some point you may need to have that particular Technician stand down and let a more senior person take over. Many times over the years I have heard, "wait, I almost have it", only to wait for another hour or two and be no further forward. Having a fresh set of eyes look at a problem can go a long way to sparking new troubleshooting ideas. Set an escalation timetable up through the various functional levels of Technicians and don't be afraid to use it.

The last key role in Incident Management is the **Help Desk**. This team can be a great help to an effective Incident Management program.

Help Desk teams are often the first to know about an incident as they may suddenly start receiving calls when something goes wrong. They can also quickly use the Incident Prioritization Matrix, discussed in Step 4, to objectively determine the correct priority of an incident and help escalate it to the correct team.

The Help Desk can also be a great source of metrics related to an incident. For example, they may be able to identify how many users are affected, what locations are reporting issues, or when an incident started. I suggest building a good relationship with this team as they are an integral part of the process.

When an incident occurs, it is also a good idea to have a Help Desk person be dedicated to that particular incident. They can be responsible for opening the incident ticket, opening the conference bridge, updating the known error database with workarounds, and eventually, closing the incident. They should also be a participant on the Incident Conference Bridge and can take on some of the workload of the Incident Manager, for example, making calls to escalate issues, or tracking details and filling out Incident Log paperwork while an incident is happening.

Lastly I wanted to talk about work schedules. One of the downfalls of a career in I.T. is that it often requires weekend and evening work. Unless you're very lucky, sooner or later you will have an incident occur during off hours. The best way to address this is to plan ahead. Set up an on-call rotation with all of your key technology teams. Make sure you know how to reach vendors after hours, and how to escalate up the appropriate management chain. Be sure to understand who will take over if staff have been working through the night and an outage is still occuring. By preparing ahead of time you can at least make the best of a very challenging situation.

I recall working for a global information company that had offices in over 150 locations. Shortly after I was hired there was a major system outage that required me to be the Incident Manager for over 30 hours straight. During this time, several of my international colleagues came and went on their regular shift, but they weren't trained in Incident Management and no formal program was in place, therefore I had to cover it. Needless to say, after I caught up on my sleep I immediately began soliciting support to impliment a global Incidement Management program!

Step 3: Incident Detection and Alerting - When It Hits the Fan!

Have you ever heard of a system being down and no one noticing it for hours, or days! It happens all the time. Often, a broken system may be overlooked as it is not used very often, or there is sufficient redundancy that the users don't notice when there is a partial failure. This can prove to be a very disasterous situation when things finally hit the fan!

Imagine a branch office that has redundant network circuits back to corporate. One circuit may be out of commision, but there may be no impact to the users due to the redundant circuit. Technically, this is still an incident as the agreed to service level (fully redundant network connectivity) is not being met. If we have good alerting set up we will know about the circuit failure and can get it resolved quickly, avoiding impact to our users.

One of the key components of a successful Incident Management program is early incident detection and appropriate alerting. There are many tools available, some even free, that can help to capture alerts from the environment and notify you when a system is down. As part of your Incident Management deployment, be sure to have all departments double-check that everything is being monitored as expected. Wherever possible, centralize these alerts into a "single pane of glass" so they are easy to watch and respond to.

Once systems are monitored, you will need to develop an alerting system that makes sense for your organization. If you are a 24x7 shop, or have colleagues around the world, be sure that your alerts go to someone who is "on the clock". Too often, an alert will go to an I.T. Technician who is not at work, or who may even be home asleep. It is critical that the moment an incident happens people are aware of it and can immediately begin the resolution process. With smartphones and text messaging, it should be relatively easy to get a custom message delivered to the right team with minimal effort.

If you don't have colleagues available 24x7, set up an on-call rotation responsible for each technology. While it is never pleasant getting a late night call about a system crash, it is better than being surprised by it as users start logging in the next morning. Another option is to consider some type of outsourced monitoring service that can evaluate an outage after hours and escalate if necessary.

This is another area the Help Desk can really be valuable. Give them access to your monitoring system and let them take a look at the incoming alerts to see if they are valid. If you're feeling bold, give I.T. Leadership access to view your alerts. You'll be surprised how often they look at them and start asking questions when something doesn't look right!

The point is that it's very important to detect an issue and get it escalated to the right people as quickly as possible. Whether it is automated (preferred), or a manual process, make sure that the alerts make sense and are prioritized properly.

One word of caution is to avoid alert overload. I.T. Techs will often talk about how they get so many alerts per day that they tend to become desensitized to them and overlook them. This defeats the purpose and is usually caused by alerts not being sent with the correct priority. Just be sure to work with your monitoring gurus and get this important piece of the puzzle set up correctly.

For additional information, check out ITIL's Event Management process where this topic is discussed in detail.

Step 4: Incident Prioritization – The Priority Scorecard

Here is the meat and potatoes of Incident Management, the Incident Prioritization Scorecard. Using a scorecard to evaluate the priority of an incident ensures that the correct response is used for the correct level of impact and urgency. Within ITIL, the following prioritization matrix is used:

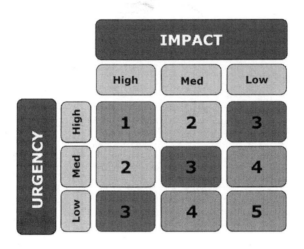

One of the challenges with ITIL's Priority Matrix is that it is very subjective and open to interpretation. ITIL revised this somewhat in the 2011 version, but it can still be improved. I suggest developing your own priority scorecard to help prioritize incidents based on your individual business needs. Also, a custom priority scorecard can help ensure incidents are evaluated objectively and in the same way, by everyone.

Let's look at an example: Assume 30 users can't access their email, how would you evaluate the priority using the ITIL scorecard? Is it a Priority 1 or a Priority 5? It becomes very difficult and is subject to too

Incident Management for I.T. Departments

much interpretation, especially if a Helpdesk person is having to decide whether to wake up the CIO in the middle of the night!

I have had good luck using a points based scoring system on my priority scorecard to determine the correct priority of an incident. Take a look at the following sample priority scorecard to see how easy this can be:

INCIDENT PRIORITY SCORECARD		
For This Incident:	**Points:**	**Points Value:**
Is more than one location impacted?		If YES, add 10 points
What percentage of employees are impacted?		20% to 74% add 10, 75% or more add 20
Is this impacting employees currently on shift?		If YES add 20 points
To what level of Executive has this issue been escalated?		Director add 10, VP add 15, C-Level add 20
Is there a redundant solution carrying the load?		If NO, add 10 points
Does this stop the ability to ship products?		If YES, add 20 points
Total Points:		

Results:
If 50 Points or More = **Priority 1** "Critical"
If 25 to 49 Points = **Priority 2** "High"
If Under 25 Points = **Priority 3** "Medium"

This type of priority scorecard can be customized for your environment. For example, you may have systems that generate revenue and that no matter what, if they are down it is a Priority 1. If so, add that into the priority scorecard so that anyone evaluating an incident will always respond appropriately.

Below is a sampling of questions that you may want included on your own priority scorecard. What makes the most sense for your business? What other questions should you be asking? How many points should each question be worth?

Take some time to run several scenarios through your own scorecard with your own scoring system and see if the resulting Incident Priority sounds correct. Based on your score, are you prioritizing an incident as a Priority 1 when it should really be a Priority 2, or vice versa? If so,

13 | P a g e

change your questions and take a few points away. It's a trial and error process, but once complete, it should be pretty accurate for just about any outage scenario.

Sample Incident Priority Questions

- Is more than one location impacted?
- What percentage of employees are impacted?
- Is this impacting employees currently on shift?
- To what level of Executive has this issue been escalated?
- Is there a redundant working system carrying the load?
- Does this stop the ability to ship products?
- Is this incident affecting the ability to generate revenue?
- Does this affect the safety and well-being of customers?
- Will this outage lead to a much larger issue if not resolved?
- Are troubleshooting experts still available if I delay resolution?
- Are there financial penalties for this system being down?
- Is this a security threat?
- Does this incident cause us to be out of compliance?
- Are we incurring extra cost while this outage is happening?
- Is this a top tier system that we all agree is always a Priority 1?

The beauty of the scorecard is that it makes prioritization very objective. This way, when a Business Unit Manager has an outage and demands you open an "all hands on deck" Priority 1 incident, you can direct him to your scorecard and help explain why his incident should really be a Priority 2 or Priority 3. Using the scorecard will help ensure you are managing your very limited resources effectively and ensuring they are focused on the highest priority tasks.

If an incident scores low, it should be responded to appropriately based on your service level agreements. Use caution against prioritizing your incidents too high, otherwise everything becomes a high priority when it doesn't need to be. Again, use your best judgement for what works in your organization.

Once you have finalized your scorecard share it with your user community and your leadership. Explain how it works and why you're using it to more effectively manage your resources. This will also help people understand what the incident score means when you publish it in your incident status notifications. You'll be pleasantly surprised how many people offer to help when an incident scores unusually high. They know this must be a severe situation and will help support you in getting resources you need to resolve the issue.

Step 5: Appropriate Response Plan – Checklists and SLA's

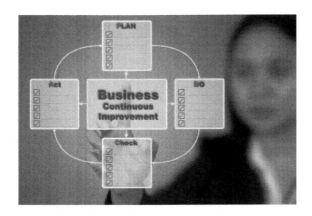

So you've got your monitoring set up and have detected an issue, alerts are going out based on your Priority Scorecard and everyone is standing by ready to help with your latest Priority 1 incident, but what exactly should they do?! This is another area where it can be very easy to get tripped up and waste a lot of time during an incident.

Too often during an outage the I.T. Department will be trying to make decisions on things that should have been planned for ahead of time. I'll give you an example; when a Priority 1 incident happens, who should be notified and what should be said? More often than not, people go looking for the highest ranking leader and ask them what to say. That person usually has very few details about the issue so valuable time is spent trying to compose a meaningful email with all the right information.

Imagine, if ahead of time there was a template developed that told you exactly what to say, when to say it and who to say it to. Makes a lot of sense, right? Does it happen in the real world, not so much!

This is where developing an appropriate Incident Management task list, along with agreed to service levels, can help. I mention service levels (SLA's) because it's an important concept in your Incident Management program. You are committing to the business that you will respond within a certain timeframe and will have a target resolution within a specific timeframe. As such, when an incident happens and you need to meet your SLA's, you will need the appropriate resources. The SLA's can help justify additional costs that are incurred to meet your committed to deadlines. For example, if your SLA states that you will continue trying to resolve a Priority 1 incident around the clock, you might need to pay for after-hours technical support on your systems.

Let's take a look at a sample Priority 1 Checklist and SLA's:

Priority 1 "Critical" — Checklist

Service Level Agreement:

> All hands on deck as soon as incident is detected
>
> Target resolution is one hour
>
> Incident is worked 24 x 7
>
> Status updates sent every 30 minutes
>
> Root cause analysis meeting within 24 hours of resolution

Specific Remediation Tasks:

> Helpdesk to acknowledge the incident and create appropriate incident ticket within 15 minutes.
>
> Helpdesk to open Incident Management Bridge immediately.
>
> Helpdesk to notify on-call I.T. Technicians and Incident Manager within 15 minutes, if no response within 5 minutes, escalate to one up manager.

Incident Manager and I.T. Technicians to assemble in the War Room, or join the Incident Management bridge immediately.

Helpdesk to begin taking notes, tracking timeline of activities and alerting as SLA breaches are approaching.

Incident Manager and I.T. Technicians to conduct basic triage and determine correct incident priority within 15 minutes.

Helpdesk to send out initial email notification to "Priority 1 Notification" email distribution list within 30 minutes.

Incident Manager to notify I.T. and Corporate Leadership based on priority and Escalation Matrix (discussed in Step 7).

I.T. Technicians to escalate issue to vendors immediately.

Incident Manager to address SLA's that have been breached with an appropriate action plan.

Helpdesk to send out updated status notification emails at 30 minute intervals.

After Issue is Resolved:

Incident Manager to send Incident Summary report to Leadership within two hours.

Incident Manager to schedule a follow-up root cause analysis meeting within 24 hours.

Incident Manager and Helpdesk to update Incident Metrics within 24 hours.

As you can see, having a detailed checklist will help ensure your teams are responding appropriately to a Priority 1 incident. There are also specific timelines called out when action needs to be taken. This helps resolve a lot of the questions that arise when something goes wrong and everyone is in panic mode. Note that this list is just a sample to give you some ideas. Use it to build on your own list and modify it to suit your company's needs.

Now let's take a look at a Priority 2 checklist and its SLA's to see how they might compare:

Priority 2 "High" — Checklist

Service Level Agreement:

Incident Manager to determine what I.T. Technicians need to be involved as soon as incident is detected

Target resolution is four hours

Incident is worked 24 hours, Monday to Friday

Status updates sent every four hours

Specific Remediation Tasks:

Helpdesk to acknowledge the incident and create appropriate incident ticket within 15 minutes.

Helpdesk to open Incident Management Bridge, if needed.

Helpdesk to notify on-call I.T. Technicians and Incident Manager within 15 minutes, if no response within 15 minutes, escalate to one up manager.

Helpdesk to begin taking notes, tracking time of activities and alerting as SLA breaches are approaching.

Incident Manager and I.T. Technicians to conduct basic triage and determine incident priority within 15 minutes.

Helpdesk to send out initial email notification to "Priority 2 Notification" email distribution list within 30 minutes.

Incident Manager to notify I.T. and Corporate Leadership based on priority and Escalation Matrix (discussed in Step 7).

I.T. Technicians to escalate issue to vendors, as needed.

Incident Manager to address SLA's that have been breached with an appropriate action plan.

Helpdesk to send out updated status notification emails at four hour intervals.

After Issue is Resolved:

Incident Manager to send Incident Summary report to Leadership within one business day.

Incident Manager to schedule a follow-up root cause analysis meeting only if needed.

Helpdesk to update Incident Metrics within 48 hours.

As you can see in the Priority 2 checklist that there is a little more "breathing room" to resolve the issue. This makes sense as it is a lower priority issue and doesn't need the all hands on deck approach that a Priority 1 needs. Again, use this as an example and customize it to suit your needs. You can also develop a Priority 3 or Priority 4 checklist from these samples so that you are fully prepared for any issue.

By creating these very repeatable checklists you save time and avoid confusion during an outage. The more detailed these lists are the less people will have to think through in an incident. You will have also laid out your service level agreements and can measure your performance against them. If you find you are not able to meet the SLA's as stated, it could be good justification for getting additional resources and making your Incident Management program even better.

Step 6: The Conference Bridge and War Room - Critical Tasks

I'm going to let you in on a little secret. The one thing that helps resolve incidents faster than anything else is having an Incident Manager take immediate ownership of the issue and drive people involved to quick resolution.

This may seem a bit obvious, but it rarely happens without a formal Incident Management program in place. What is more common is that a system will go down and people will start wandering the hallways looking to see who else is having the same problem. Usually, the first sign of a major incident is a group of I.T. Technicians huddled around one person's desk, all looking very anxious, but not quite sure what to do.

Developing your Incident Management program will help everyone understand what their role is and what the expectations are. They can then quickly follow this plan and begin taking steps to resolve the outage.

As mentioned in Step 4, using a Priority Scorecard will help determine the appropriate priority, and more importantly, the appropriate response to an incident. As we saw in Step 5, you should have a clearly defined checklist, including SLA's, that start the moment an outage is detected.

Let's assume that your Helpdesk has received several calls and a major application has gone down. They've used the Priority Scorecard and have rated the outage a "Priority 1". What should happen next?

The most important thing for everyone to remember is that if it's a Priority 1, that means "all hands on deck". Every key person in I.T. needs to be ready to participate. As an example, even if it is obviously a network problem, you still need the Server and Application teams to assess the impact and be ready to restart systems as appropriate.

Now is not the time to be concerned about calling people at home, or asking people to come in to the office to help. This should have already been planned for with your On-Call rotation. By getting buy-in from Management for your Incident Management program up front, plus clearly communicating the expectations, you should be comfortable that you can call whomever is needed to resolve the outage, without repurcussions.

Another best practice is to have a designated conference room that can become your "War Room" during an incident. You should post a sign on the wall that this room may be taken over at any time for Incident Management purposes, even if another meeting is underway. Try to pick a room with a projector and large whiteboard as you will be sharing a lot of information.

A designated Incident Conference Bridge should also be set up. Again, don't wait to get this taken care of, and don't share this conference number for other purposes. Designate it just for Incident Management and enourage everyone to memorize how to use it. I've often seen this bridge number taped to the back of employee badges, or printed on a business card that everyone can keep handy. It is also helpful to create an Outlook contact with these details and send it to everyone that needs it.

The moment you learn about an incident two things should happen. First, the War Room should be commandeered and everyone should be asked to move to that room. I.T. Technicians are often hesitant to do this as they are most comfortable working at their desks, but the benefits of having everyone in one room discussing the outage far outweigh the advantages of working in isolation.

The second thing that should happen is that everyone should join the Incident Conference bridge, including vendors. If your conference bridge supports break out sessions, that is even better. If not, you may need a second conference bridge that is set up for communication with the business and user community.

The conference bridge should be hosted by the Incident Manager and there should be an agreed to protocol. For example, nothing is more distracting that people constantly joining the bridge and wanting a "quick update". You should establish up front that status updates will be given at certain intervals, or via email or chat sessions. This way the bridge can be left open for communcation between the participants that are resolving the outage.

The reason I mention vendors should be included on the bridge is that too often a technician will be talking with a vendor on a separate call, while simultaneously trying to share what is happening. It is much more productive to have the vendor on the main bridge where everyone can hear what is going on and ask additional questions. Time and again this has led to someone asking, "Have we tried XYZ?", which often leads to the resolution.

Another important task for the Incident Manager is to ensure that forward progress is being made. The Incident Manager needs to understand who is working on what, and what the current roadblock is. They should be calling out current activities and making sure everyone is working quickly to get the outage resolved. Again, people that are not shy about challenging others and driving for results make great Incident Managers!

The next step for the Incident Manager is to start tracking everything on a white board. This should include a timeline as each activity happens, plus a list of known issues. It may also be helpful to track what has been changed during troubleshooting as this will be important information in the root cause analysis phase.

Useful Whiteboard Information:
- Incident Bridge number
- Problem description and systems involved
- Initial and current impact
- Timeline of events throughout the incident
- Potential causes being investigated
- Changes and corrective actions
- Vendors involved
- Additional notes

A few other things to keep in mind regarding the Incident Bridge and War Room. You may have international participants, so be sure to use dial in numbers that are supported in their countries. It may also be helpful to video conference with others while troubleshooting. A picture is worth a thousand words!

Lastly, the Incident Manager should be the only person who can allow a technician to hang up from the bridge. It is common for a technician to dial in, quickly decide that this doesn't affect their technology and then drop off, only to be needed a few minutes later. Only when an Incident Manager is fully comfortable that a person is no longer needed, should they be allowed to hang up.

Again, effective conference bridge and War Room management is one of the most critical pieces of Incident Management.

Step 7: The Escalation Matrix – Who and When to Escalate

Imagine a Priority 2 incident has just happened. Who should be called immediately? When should the issue be escalated to a Director or VP? Should the CIO ever be notified? After an outage, have you ever heard the phrase, "Nobody told me, I could have fixed it"?

A common concern in I.T. is how and when to escalate. No one is ever really sure when to alert the CIO, or even more daunting, the other C-Level leaders in the company. Should they be told about all Priority 1's, or just certain Priority 1's that have very major impact?

The good news is that there's an easy way to resolve this. Again, the best approach is to plan ahead and establish the ground rules for exactly what happens, and at what time interval, during an outage.

I suggest creating an **Escalation Matrix** that everyone is aware of and has agreed to. It should state the action items for each priority of incident and the time that they should happen. This way it is never subjective as to whether or not to alert senior level colleagues.

By using an Escalation Matrix, even the most junior employee can determine exactly when to call their Manager, their Director, or the CIO. Given that everyone has agreed to this matrix, there should be no guilt about waking someone up in the middle of the night to alert them of a situation.

Let's take a look at an example Escalation Matrix:

Contact	Timeframe	Priority 1	Priority 2	Priority 3
IT Helpdesk	At time of incident	Informed	Informed	Informed
IT Technicians	At time of incident	Informed	Informed	Informed
IT Senior Engineers	At time of incident	Informed	As Needed	Not Informed
Vendors	At time of incident	Informed	As Needed	As Needed
IT Managers	At time of incident	Informed	As Needed	Not Informed
IT Directors	At time of incident	Informed	As Needed	Not Informed
IT CIO	At time of incident	As Needed	Not Informed	Not Informed
IT Senior Engineers	After 2 Hours	Updated	Informed	As Needed
Vendors	After 2 Hours	Updated	As Needed	As Needed
IT Managers	After 2 Hours	Updated	As Needed	Not Informed
IT Directors	After 2 Hours	Updated	As Needed	Not Informed
IT CIO	After 2 Hours	As Needed	Not Informed	Not Informed
IT Senior Engineers	After 4 Hours	Updated	Updated	As Needed
Vendors	After 4 Hours	Updated	As Needed	As Needed
IT Managers	After 4 Hours	Updated	Informed	Not Informed
IT Directors	After 4 Hours	Updated	As Needed	Not Informed
IT CIO	After 4 Hours	Informed	Not Informed	Not Informed

In this Escalation Matrix we can see that as soon as a Priority 1 incident occurs, everyone, except the CIO is notified. The CIO will be notified as needed based on his or her preferences. In a Priority 2 incident, the Helpdesk and I.T. Technicians are informed right away, but others are involved only as needed. If the Priority 2 issue persists, I.T. Senior Engineers are informed at the two hour mark and other people are escalated to on an as needed basis.

In this matrix we are assuming that the same notification schedule happens 24x7. If your company doesn't have round the clock support you may want to have a weekday and weekend matrix that are slightly different.

The Escalation Matrix can be customized to meet your needs. The important thing is to share it and get buy-in from all levels. You may find your CIO wants to be notified at the moment any Priority 1 happens. If so, that is great! Update the matrix accordingly and make sure your Incident Management teams are following that directive.

Step 8: The Communication Plan – Spread the Word

When an incident happens it's very important to ensure the right people know what is going on as quickly as possible. They must be kept apprised of the situation as things change, or as the impact is reduced. For I.T. leaders it can be frustrating to have to keep contacting your I.T. team to see what the status is. Likewise, from an I.T. Technician's standpoint, it is distracting to have to keep repeating the same status verbiage to multiple people.

The right thing to do is to create your communication plan and appropriate templates ahead of time. This way, in the heat of battle you are not trying to compose a meaningful message that might be seen by all employees. Instead, you can stay focused on finding the cause of the outage and fixing it. By planning ahead, you can prepare an Incident Notification template for each incident priority. This way, you will know exactly what to say, who to send it to and when to send it.

When thinking about your communication plan, think who really needs to know about each type of incident. What do they need to know, and how often. Should it be sent via email, a voicemail broadcast, text alerts, or should phone calls be made? You will probably find a combination approach works best. For example, if it is a Priority 1, don't just rely on an email, especially after hours. Make sure you call and make contact with key people who need to be kept in the loop.

Developing the plan will require input from many of your colleagues, both within I.T. and in the business. An incident not only impacts systems, but may impact key processes in your business. Your business colleagues may need to make significant changes to their operations as a result of a system being down, so be sure to include them in your Communication Plan discussions.

Let's consider an example. Imagine that a Sales Order report failed to run overnight. Your business customers will have no idea what to ship, who to invoice, or what replacement inventory should be ordered. However. if they are part of your Communication Plan they will know about the outage and can take steps to remediate the situation.

While the verbiage of phone calls or text messages should be pretty straight forward, the email communication requires quite a bit of thought. You want your message to answer all the likely questions that anyone involved might ask. It also needs to be concise and readable on various device types. Following is an email template I have used successfully in the past. It can be updated and resent throughout the life of an incident. As you can see, it contains all the relevent pieces of information needed in an incident. For example, it shows the initial incident impact, plus the current incident impact. Over time, the impact may lessen as issues are resolved. It can be helpful to call this out in the status update messages.

Incident Notifcation Email Template

Incident Notification: Initial / **Update** / Close			
Priority: P1	**Points:** 75	**Notification Time:** 7:45 AM	**Ticket:** 161423
Incident Bridge: Tel **1-555-1212**, Conference ID: **020289**			
Incident Description: Sales Order processing server unexpectedly shut down causing the Sales Order workflow to stop.			
Initial Incident Impact: Unable to process new sales orders			
Current Incident Impact: Accounting cannot produce invoices. Today's shipments are being delayed until tomorrow. Inventory orders have been cancelled.			
Incident Workaround: None at this time			
Business Units Impacted: Manufacturing **Departments Impacted:** Sales, Accounts Payable, Shipping **Locations Impacted:** Los Angeles, Denver **Number of Employees Impacted:** 100 **Revenue Impacting:** Yes **Incident Manager:** John Smith **Resolution Owner:** Server Team			
Status Updates: 9:30 am: Second server is coming online, anticipate resolution by 10:00 am 9:00 am: Failing over to second server and will reprocess Sales Order workflow 8:30 am: Server team is troubleshooting failed server with vendors assistance 8:00 am: Server vendor has joined the Incident Bridge 7:50 am: Incident Management process initiated, Incident Bridge opened 7:45 am: Initial issue reported by the business			
Incident Close Time: pending			

This template also shows things like locations impacted and number of employees impacted. Going back to your Priority Scorecard, from Step 4, you may want to include those questions and answers here too. Customize it to make the most sense for your business needs. After you send it out a few times solicit feedback and see if it is conveying the right information to your user community.

Your Response Plan and Service Level Agreements, created in Step 5, will tell you how often to send out these updates. In our sample plan, we have stated that status updates on a Priority 1 Incident will be sent every 30 minutes. Therefore, we need to be sure this message is being sent out in a timely fashion that meets this requirement.

To make things easier, I suggest creating a "Priority 1 Notification" email distribution list. Add everyone to this list that wants to be notified during a Priority 1 Incident. Whenever a Priority 1 Incident happens simply fill out this template and email it to this distribution list. Very simple! Of course, you'll still want to make calls to key people, but this email will help spread the word to the majority of people who are interested, but not necessarily directly involved, in your incident. I suggest also creating a "Priority 2 Notification" and "Priority 3 Notification" distribution list.

Another consideration is who to send this message to. It contains detailed information about the troubleshooting steps and possible impact. I have seen cases where Management is ok with this going to I.T. staff, but doesn't want this type of detail going to customers. If that is the case, create a second template that is more generic for those customers. Again, take the templates provided here and adjust them to meet your needs. No need to reinvent the wheel! Keep your processes simple, efficient and repeatable, especially during a crisis.

Step 9: Vendor Management – Expect Great Service

I can't tell you how many times over the years a vendor has saved the day during an incident! While it seems that I.T. costs soar every year while the vendor sharks circle in a feeding frenzy, take advantage of this spend and really get your money's worth.

What I'm suggesting here is to build really good relationships with your vendors. Treat them like a valued partner and not just a supplier. Get to know your vendor's Sales Reps, and more importantly, their Engineers. It's also icing on the cake to get to know their leadership team. In the event of a major outage you might need to escalate a few rungs up the vendor's management ladder to get the response you need.

Here's an example of how this can be a win-win for everyone involved. During a recent, large hardware purchase I had the vendor include some professional services to help with the installation. My goal was two fold, first, to ensure it was installed correctly while my team learned the system, but secondly to make sure the vendor had some skin in the game. If the system failed, which it subsequently did, the vendor was up to speed on how it was set up and was willing to provide some free onsite technical support given that I had spent so much money with them. Overall, they made a little extra money with some professional services during the sale, and I got a little piece of mind knowing they would help out in an incident.

Don't be shy about asking a vendor for assistance when you are dealing with an issue. It's all part of having a good relationship with them and building a partnership. Often, they will have some hardware to loan you, or may have extra clout with other vendors that are involved. Of course, when the dust settles, be prepared to hear all about how they rescued you and how you should buy more product from them! Fair enough, if they were there during a major incident, send some business their way as a thank you.

Let's also discuss the flip side to vendor relationships, when a vendor doesn't perform as expected. This is one of the few times when it is actually ok to have what I'll call "heated" discussions with your vendors. Given that you probably spend very large sums with your vendors you should expect first class service. Anything less, especially in a crisis, should result in you having strong conversations with the vendor's management team.

After an incident where a vendor hasn't performed, set up a meeting with them to discuss their response. Be sure to give them the opportunity to explain their situation, but also ask for appropriate credit, or goodwill, on a future purchase. It may also help to suggest ways they can improve their response. They are trying to earn your business, so don't be afraid to hold them to a very high standard. Even sharing some of the basic incident management steps taught in this book can help a vendor with poor processes to improve.

Step 10: Go Live - Training, Testing and Documentation

Now that we've covered the steps to design your Incident Management program, how do we actually put it into practice and bring it to life?

The first key step is to meet with your colleagues and talk through what works for your company. Run through many different incident scenarios and see what should be included and what can be left out. From experience, the steps laid out in this book are very common across most organizations. Therefore, begin to build off of the various templates and guidelines included here to kickstart your program.

Now that you have a concept of what your program will look like, take it to leadership and solicit their buy-in. Be sure to articulate the value of faster incident resolution and less impact to the business. With a well thought out business plan they should be fully on board. With their support you can then develop an implementation plan. Set goals and timelines for each stage of your rollout and put together a formal project plan. This will help ensure a smooth transition to your new Incident Management program.

Once you have the structure of your program, develop an in-house training program to share the concepts with others. This is an important step as it helps get everyone involved and gets them comfortable with their roles. It may also make sense to have key participants attend formal training. ITIL's Foundation level program is ideal to get people introduced to basic I.T. best practices and methodologies, including Incident Management. For more specific troubleshooting and incident resolution training, take a look at third party companies like Kepner-Tregoe.

With your leadership supporting you and your teams trained, now is the time to test your program. First, look at your past incidents for the year and run them through the program. How would they have scored on the Priority Matrix? Would your response plan have been appropriate for that type of incident? Did you escalate to the right people? Were vendors involved when needed? By answering these questions with real world incidents you will get a very good feel for how you've set up your program. If it's not quite right adjust the scores up or down a bit and try again. Before long, you will have it fine tuned and will be ready to go live!

The last piece of the puzzle is documentation. Not always the funnest part of I.T. but definitely very important. There are several important documents you need to include in your documentation set. You also need to determine who will own them and keep them updated. This should be worked out and agreed to as you develop your Incident Management program.

Things You Will Need to Document

- **Incident Priority Matrix**—Where does it live? Can it be automated on a web page or on a spreadsheet? Can the scoring be included as a record in the Incident Ticket for tracking purposes? This needs to be readily available for everyone to use and understand. Include some sample incident scorecards as a reference.

- **Response Plans**—Document detailed step-by-step instructions that will be followed in an incident. Everyone will be using this response plan during an outage so it needs to be accurate and make sense. The more detailed it is, the less you will need to work out during a crisis. This is also where you will have defined your SLA's so make sure you are holding the team accountable to these commitments.

- **Escalation Matrix**—This is your go to list of how to escalate up the organizational chart. Be sure to have everyone's agreement on this one and make sure it is readily available during an outage. Also, determine and document up front who will call each of these people. This is where the Helpdesk can be really useful, have them make the calls while the Incident Manager stays focused on resolving the incident. Also, keep in mind you may need a different Escalation Matrix for weekend or holidays if you are not a 24x7 shop.

- **On-Call Schedule**—An easy one to overlook, but very important. You need to know who is responsible for each technology 24x7. Create a centralized on-call schedule for all I.T. departments that is updated weekly. This can then be quickly referenced when issues need to be escalated. One tip is to investigate some of the calendaring tools that incorporate an on-call schedule. Some will even tie into an alerting system so that notifications go to the correct person automatically, even during vacations.

- **I.T. Contact List**—Be sure to have a current contact list for everyone in I.T. plus any key business colleagues. Nothing is worse that trying to call a Manager in the middle of the night only to find you have the wrong number! Also, note if there are any international dialing instructions if you have global colleagues. I also suggest having the phone numbers and addresses of all your branch offices documented here, just in case a vendor needs to come onsite. While a lot of contact information can be stored in email or Active Directory, I like to keep this list in a simple document on my phone, just in case the outage prevents me from getting to my contacts online.

- **Vendor List**—Keep a current list of all vendors and who the Sales, Engineering and Leadership staff are from that business. Also, include information like support contract numbers, circuit ID's, after-hours support agreements etc.

- **Product List**—If you don't have a Configuration Management Database (CMDB) available, at least keep a list of all your applications, product information and any dependancies. For example, assume you use Oracle for your ERP system. Keep track of who supports that product within your company, plus what the impact is if that product goes down. This will be important for evaluating the true impact of an outage.

- **Metrics**—Determine what metrics you are going to measure for each incident and how you are going to track and report them. Are you going to consider an incident resolved once there is no user impact, or when the full system is back to 100% capacity? Are you going to track details like how quickly various teams responded to you opening an Incident Bridge? Lots to think about. Discussing these metrics with Management on a regular basis will help improve performance of all teams involved.

- **Known Error Database**—At the end of each incident think about what all went into your resolution. What steps were taken to troubleshoot and diagnose the problem? What workarounds were implemented that helped lessen the impact to the user community? Be sure to document these in your Known Error Database (KEDB) so that they can be used again if the same issue happens in the future.

- **Incident Summary**—After each Priority 1 incident it is very helpful to send out an Incident Summary report to all involved, including leadership. This should include a description of what happened, the impact, timeline, people involved, relevant metrics, root cause, and any lessons learned.

- **Team Responsibilities List**—Lastly, it is always good to keep a list of each I.T. team and what products and systems they are responsible for. For example, does the Network team take care of the firewalls, or is that the Security team? When a system crashes this will be one of the first places you look to see who can help.

I've see cases where all of these documents are contained in a single spreadsheet. I've also seen it hosted on an elaborate website that has some automated updates. The point is that it needs to be kept fresh and be readily available to anyone that needs it.

Once these last few action items are completed you are ready to go live with your Incident Management program! Best of luck as you role it out, I'm confident higher customer satisfaction is headed your way!

Sample Templates

Escalation Matrix—Used to determine appropriate time for functional and hierarchical escalations:

ESCALATION MATRIX				
Contact	Timeframe	Priority 1	Priority 2	Priority 3
IT Helpdesk	At time of incident			
IT Technicians	At time of incident			
IT Senior Engineers	At time of incident			
Vendors	At time of incident			
IT Managers	At time of incident			
IT Directors	At time of incident			
IT CIO	At time of incident			
IT Senior Engineers	After 2 Hours			
Vendors	After 2 Hours			
IT Managers	After 2 Hours			
IT Directors	After 2 Hours			
IT CIO	After 2 Hours			
IT Senior Engineers	After 4 Hours			
Vendors	After 4 Hours			
IT Managers	After 4 Hours			
IT Directors	After 4 Hours			
IT CIO	After 4 Hours			

On Call Schedule—Make sure each technology is listed and you have 24x7 coverage identified.

IT ON CALL SCHEDULE						
	Week:	Incident Manager	Servers	Databases	Networking	Storage
Jan 1 - Jan 7	6:00 AM to 6:00 PM PST	Andrew Stoller	Jonas Hambrick	Kurt Nokes	Danny Boxx	Wanda Wolery
	6:00 PM to 6:00 AM PST	Kristina Deckert	Justine Steil	Thom Tellis	Vick Earnhardt	Abdul Byrne
Jan 8 - Jan 15	6:00 AM to 6:00 PM PST	Stan Angus	Dan Hershner	Cleve Phifer	Kenya Weldon	Nick Judson
	6:00 PM to 6:00 AM PST	Cathy Trigg	Gemma Taub	Trinity Robson	Russel Dolby	Sheryl Clyne

Product List—Be sure that all products and systems you support are included. Note any information that will be helpful in an incident:

PRODUCT LIST:				
Product:	IT Contact:	Vendor:	Vendor Contact:	Notes:
Physical Servers	Jonas Hambrick	Dell	Clare Otani	May need to contact HP for some hardware
Unix Servers	Justine Steil	HP	Rob Buser	We have 24x7 on all these systems
Virtual Servers	Dan Hershner	VMware	Arnette Kinsey	Gemma can also back Dan up on these
Telecom	Danny Boxx	Avaya	Al Germain	Al's backup is Kelly Peterson
Network Routers	Vick Earnhardt	Cisco	Kim Lablanc	Call Cisco or CDW for these issues
Databases	Kurt Nokes	Oracle	Nick McCarroll	For SQL talk to Kurt first

Incident Summary Report—This goes out after an incident has occurred and gives a detailed summary of what happened and how it was resolved.

INCIDENT SUMMARY REPORT	
Outage Start Date/Time:	
Outage End Date/Time:	
Incident Ticket:	
Incident Manager:	
Incident Description:	
Initial Priority:	
Final Priority:	
Incident Score:	
Customer Impact:	
System Impact:	
Resolution Steps:	
5 Whys?	
RCA Conclusion:	
Follow Up Items:	
Lessons Learned:	

Incident Notification Email—This should be sent out multiple times while an incident is occuring. Add status updates as needed.

INCIDENT NOTIFICATION: Initial / Update / Close			
Priority:	Points:	Notification Time:	Ticket:
Incident Bridge Tel: Conference ID:			
Incident Description:			
Initial Incident Impact:			
Current Incident Impact:			
Incident Workaround:			
Business Units Impacted:			
Departments Impacted:			
Locations Impacted:			
Number of Employees Impacted:			
Revenue Impacting:			
Incident Manager:			
Resolution Owner:			
Status Updates:			
Incident Close Time:			

Conclusion and Thanks

You have now seen how easy it can be to create your own Incident Management program. The important things to remember are to get everyone on board with the plan, prioritize incidents correctly, respond quickly and drive for resolution! In no time you will see positive impacts from your efforts. Customer satisfaction will go up, productivity will go up and you may end up getting some well deserved kudos for how you are creating a stable and well managed environment.

I would like to personally thank you for taking time to read this book. Information Technology has been a passion of mine for the last 30 years and has been a very enjoyable career. I hope you find it just as compelling and rewarding.

Best Regards,

Darren O'Toole

Darren_OToole@Advantiga.com

Made in the USA
Middletown, DE
08 February 2016